This Is a Let's-Read-and-Find-Out Science Book®

ALL KINDS OF FEET

Ron and Nancy Goor

Thomas Y. Crowell | New York

The *Let's-Read-and-Find-Out Science Book* series was originated by Dr. Franklyn M. Branley, Astronomer Emeritus and former Chairman of The American Museum-Hayden Planetarium, and was formerly co-edited by him and Dr. Roma Gans, Professor Emeritus of Childhood Education, Teachers College, Columbia University.

Let's-Read-and-Find-Out Science Book is a registered trademark of Harper & Row, Publishers, Inc.

Library of Congress Cataloging in Publication Data
Goor, Ron.
  All kinds of feet.

  (Let's-read-and-find-out science book)
  Summary: Text and photographs present the different
types of feet found in the animal kingdom and describe how
each type is specifically suited to the needs of the
particular animal to which it belongs.
  1. Foot—Juvenile literature [1. Foot] I. Goor,
Nancy. II. Title. III. Series.
QL950.7.G66 1984   599′.049   83-45239
ISBN 0-690-04384-8
ISBN 0-690-04385-6 (lib. bdg.)

2 3 4 5 6 7 8 9 10   Designed by Al Cetta

Your feet are just right for the jobs they do. Your heel is padded. It cushions your steps. Your arch gives your foot spring as you walk. Your toes dig in and help you stand and walk. Try walking without using your toes.

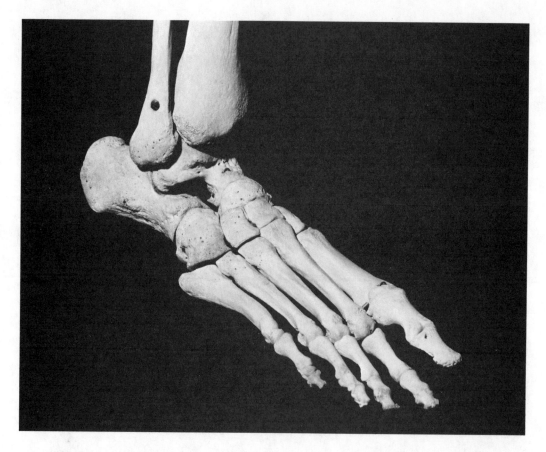

You have 26 bones in each foot, and 20 muscles. They work together so you can walk and run, skip, hop, and jump. Your feet also hold up your body.

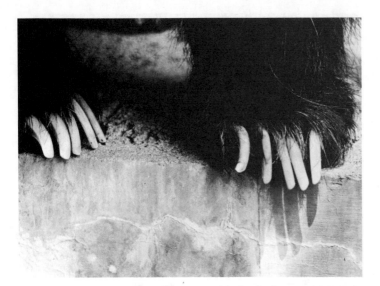 

Other animals also have feet that are just right for the things they do. They have paws for digging, webbed feet for swimming, and hoofs for galloping. They have special feet that help them live in special places.

A camel has big, flat feet with only two toes. A pad that can stretch connects the toes. When a camel walks, its toes spread far apart. Wide feet keep the camel from sinking into the loose sand. Leathery soles protect the camel's feet from getting burned by the hot desert sand.

Polar bears live where there is always snow and ice. Their broad, flat feet keep them from sinking into the soft snow. The bottoms of their feet are covered with fur to keep them from slipping. A polar bear's strong claws dig into the ice and help it climb onto icebergs.

The foot of a sea lion doesn't even look like a foot. It looks like a paddle. But it is a foot. Inside there are five toes. Flesh and skin have grown over the toes and between them. This makes a flipper that's just right for swimming.

Koalas have feet made for climbing. They have long, sharp nails to grab onto branches. Each front foot has two thumbs for an extra-sure grip. The second and third toes of each back foot are joined together into one toe, which has two claws. Koalas comb their own hair and groom each other with these special claws.

A two-toed sloth also has feet made for climbing. It has two large, curved claws on its front feet, and three big claws on its back feet. It hooks its claws onto a branch and hangs upside down. A sloth rarely leaves its home in the trees. It is hard to walk on the ground with such long, hooked claws.

Squirrels have sharp, curved claws, too. They can run straight up and down trees. They can even hang upside down by their back feet while holding an acorn in their front paws.

Squirrels have feet made for climbing.

Zebras have feet for running. They have thick, hard hoofs to protect their feet from rough ground. Hoofs are really toenails. Zebras walk on tiptoe, on their toenails. Zebras have only one toe on each foot. This makes their feet lighter. Light feet and long legs help zebras run fast.

These animals have hoofed feet, too.

Their feet are also made for running.

Birds have front feet that are very different from
their back feet.

Their back feet may have webbed toes for swimming
or standing in mud.

They may have grasping toes for perching on
branches or long, thin toes for walking on mud or sand.

Their front legs and feet are wings for flying.

Next time you eat chicken, look at the wing. You'll find the bones of a leg and a foot with three toes. The thumb and pinky are missing.

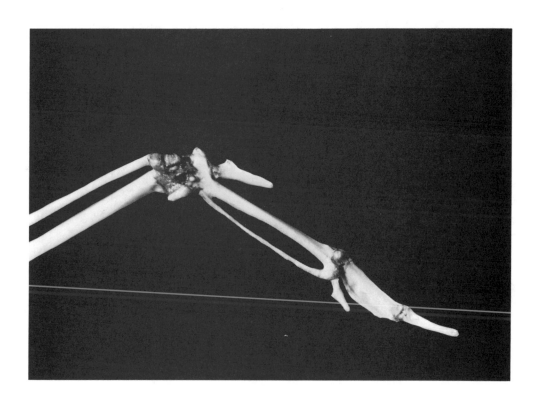

Bats also have feet made for flying. Their wings are made of skin stretched between the toes of their front feet. Four long, thin toe bones act like the frame of an umbrella. They spread out and give the wing shape. A thumb sticks out from each of the bat's wings. It helps the bat climb trees and hang from the walls of caves.

Animals have feet that help them move around in different ways. But feet do more than that. Feet help animals get food.

Anteaters use four long, curved claws to rip open anthills. In one day an anteater can lick up 30,000 ants with its long, sticky tongue. An anteater cannot walk on its claws. They are too long and get in the way. The claws are folded in, and the anteater walks on its knuckles.

Tigers' claws are hidden between the soft pads of their feet. The claws make no noise when a tiger walks, so it can sneak up on its prey. When a tiger pounces, its curved claws come out. They help the tiger grab and hold whatever it catches. Other cats have the same kind of claws.

Digging feet. Killing feet. Feet help animals get food. But feet do more than that. They help animals protect themselves and escape from danger.

An ostrich is a bird, but it cannot fly. Even though an ostrich can run fast, it cannot always run away from its enemies. Sometimes it must fight. An ostrich has powerful legs and feet for kicking. Its sharp, strong nails can slice through the hide of a lion.

An armadillo's body and head are covered with hard, bony plates. But the underside of its body is soft and unprotected. When it is being chased, an armadillo can quickly dig a hole with its strong, shovel-like front claws. It kicks out the dirt with its wide back claws. Out flies the dirt, and soon the armadillo is buried inside.

Kicking feet. Digging feet. Animals have special feet to protect them from their enemies.

There is an animal whose front feet make it different from all other animals. This animal can dig deep ditches without long, sharp claws. It can speed through water but has no flippers.

It can race across hard ground for hours but has no hoofs. It can fly, but it has no wings. This special animal is you.

Unlike other animals, you need only your back feet to move around. Your front feet are free to do other things. Your front feet are called hands.

Your hands are just right for driving cars and boats and backhoes. They are just right for making and using tools, for writing and drawing, for tying shoelaces, playing the piano, and doing much more.

Your back feet are just right for standing, walking, running, or jumping.

The feet of other animals are just right for the things they must do.

The next time you visit a zoo, you'll see the special feet that animals have. And you'll be able to figure out how they use them.